ASTROLOGY IN MEDICINE

ASTROLOGY IN MEDICINE

THE FITZPATRICK LECTURES
DELIVERED BEFORE
THE ROYAL COLLEGE OF PHYSICIANS
ON
NOVEMBER 6 AND 11, 1913
WITH ADDENDUM ON
SAINTS AND SIGNS

by

CHARLES ARTHUR MERCIER,

M.D.

FELLOW OF THE COLLEGE

GYAN

Published by

GYAN

Gyan Publishing House
5, Ansari Road
Daryaganj, New Delhi-110002
Phone: 011-47034999, 9811692060
E-mail: books@gyanbooks.com

Distribution Network
gyanbooks.com
India, USA, Canada, UK, Australia, France

ISBN : 978-81-212-6010-7 (PB)
First Published, 1914

2nd Impression 2021

Printed at: Gyan Press, Delhi.

Astrology in Medicine
Author: Charles Arthur Mercier

ASTROLOGY IN MEDICINE

THE FITZPATRICK LECTURES

DELIVERED BEFORE
THE ROYAL COLLEGE OF PHYSICIANS
ON
NOVEMBER 6 AND 11, 1913

WITH ADDENDUM ON

SAINTS AND SIGNS

BY

CHARLES ARTHUR MERCIER, M.D.
FELLOW OF THE COLLEGE

MACMILLAN AND CO., LIMITED
ST. MARTIN'S STREET, LONDON
1914

TO

SIR THOMAS BARLOW, Bart., K.C.V.O.

PRESIDENT OF THE ROYAL COLLEGE OF PHYSICIANS OF LONDON

CONTENTS

LECTURE I

THE position of Astrology among the Sciences is quite unique. Its origin is so remote as to antecede all written records: it has formed an important part of the life of every nation that has advanced beyond barbarism: it has been studied with enthusiasm not only by every European nation, but also by the Egyptians, the natives of India, the Chinese, the Arabs, the Jews, and by the Babylonians and the Chaldeans. It was studied in one long unbroken effort for thousands of years, and engaged the most strenuous endeavours of some of the greatest intellects in every age. Albertus Magnus was a convinced astrologer, and even Roger Bacon, that very great man, projected a universal medicine founded upon Astrology. A knowledge of Astrology was a necessary part of the equipment of all educated men; and Astrological terms form to this day an integral part of every European language. We still *consider*; we still find persons and things *in opposition*; we still suffer *disaster*; we still find some things *exorbitant*; and others in the *ascendent*; some persons are still fortunate enough to be born *under a lucky star*; we still deal in *merchandise*; with *merchants*; we are all familiar with the *martial* cloak of Sir J. Moore; we still describe dispositions and persons as *Saturnine, Jovial, Martial* or *Mercurial*; we still retain the names of *Saturday, Sunday* and *Monday*; in Medicine we retain the terms *Lunatic* and *Venereal disease,* and in the latter we still prescribe *Mercury*; and we still begin our prescriptions with the sign of *Jupiter.*

Yet these are the only remaining remnants of a science and an art that were once of paramount importance; and even medical men are ignorant of the very terminology of a science and an art that have been declared, by authority after authority, to be so necessary to the proper practice of medicine, that without them medicine could not be efficiently practised, and no medical practitioner was fully equipped for his task. Astrology is now utterly extinct. It began to decay at the renaissance; it languished in the seventeenth century; the last man of high distinction who practised it in this country was John Dryden[1]; but though Peter Woulfe, a F.R.S., maintained the truth of Astrology at the beginning of the nineteenth century, it had really expired when it received its deathblow from the biting humour of Jonathan Swift. Yet when Walter Scott, less than a century afterwards, introduced into one of his novels the terms of the art, there was no one then living, nor has there been since any commentator of sufficient knowledge, to expose the blunders that he made.

To such a record there is no parallel in the history of human endeavour. There are indeed two subjects of study that afford an approximation, but an approximation only, to the history of Astrology. The first of these is Alchemy, which really included what we now call Chemistry, and

[1] In a letter to his sons John and Charles, dated Sept. 3, 1697, Dryden says 'Towards the latter end of this month, September, Charles will begin to recover his perfect health according to his nativity, which, casting it myself, I am sure is true, and all things hitherto have happened according to the very time that I predicted them.' See also the Preface to his Fables, and the lines

> The utmost malice of the stars is past—
> Now frequent trines the happier lights among,
> And high raised Jove, from his dark prison freed,
> Those weights took off that on his planet hung,
> Will gloriously the new-laid works succeed.

is therefore very far from extinct. Alchemy is usually, however, understood to mean solely, what it did in fact include as its principal objects, the search for the philosopher's stone, and the search for the elixir of life. The philosopher's stone was desired, not as an end in itself, but as a means to the transmutation of metals, which were not then known to be elements. I need not remind this audience that this endeavour, which has been the object for the finger of scorn for so many years, is now almost within sight of success. Certain elements are now transmuted, or transmute themselves; and one at least of the metals known to the ancient Alchemists is now made in the laboratory. Nor need I remind you that one eminent physician discovered, a few years ago, the elixir of life in orchidian extract; while another has still more recently made the surprising discovery that the elixir of life is neither more nor less than sour milk. He was more fortunate than a predecessor, who first isolated alcohol, and having drunk freely of the newly discovered elixir of life, died, by the irony of fate, of acute alcoholic poisoning.

A nearer parallel to the fate of Astrology is to be found in that of Aristotelian Logic; but the parallel is still not quite complete. It is true that Logic was once cultivated with the same universality and the same fervour as Astrology; that it was aforetime, like Astrology, a necessary part of the equipment of every man who pretended to be educated; and that it is now fallen into neglect and contempt that are well-nigh as universal as its former cultivation; but, unlike Astrology, Logic is not yet quite extinct. It is dying, indeed: it is in the very agony of death: but it still breathes. The lamp of Astrology is utterly gone out, but the expiring flame of Logic still flickers precariously in some of the dark places of the earth. We might still find, by diligent search, professors who know the meaning of Barbara and Celarent, of Bocardo and Baralipton, and can even subject them to the orthodox manipulations of logical art; but who now knows the meaning of a triplicity or a horoscope? or could cast a geniture, or rectify a nativity? Logic is moribund, it is true, but Astrology is already dead. It has been dead so long that it no longer stinks; perhaps because it is embalmed in the writings of so many men that were eminent in their day. We have even forgotten how conspicuous and important a position it occupied among the sciences, the arts, and the crafts of our forefathers; and it is because the long sleep of medicine, its stagnation and want of progress through so many centuries, was due in no small degree to the shackles of Astrology, and of the humoral pathology, which Astrology countenanced and corroborated, that I think it seemly and proper to bring before this College the elementary principles of Astrology, and the ways in which they were applied to medicine.

Astrology had a known history of nearly six thousand years. Its beginning seems to have been in Chaldea about 4000 B.C.: it was diffused throughout all nations and peoples that had any pretence to civilisation; and it engaged, throughout that immense time and that enormous area, the attention of innumerable votaries, among whom were some of the greatest intellects that have adorned the human race. It had consequently attained to a degree of elaboration and complexity which renders it difficult to give, within any reasonable compass, a clear account of its voluminous details, expressed as they are in highly technical terminology, and conveyed in Latin so canine and so extraordinarily abbreviated as to be obscure, often to the point of unintelligibility. In preparing the account that I shall give, I have had the advantage of appealing on different points, to a Latin scholar of rare attainments, to a Professor of Astronomy, and to a Professor of Ancient History, and I rejoice to say that one and all have been unable to solve some of the problems that had puzzled myself. Where such solar luminaries have failed to illuminate, it is no disgrace to my farthing candle if it gives no light.

The main factors in Astrology are three:—the Signs of the Zodiac, the Seven Planets, and the Houses of Heaven[1].

In Medical Astrology there is yet another factor, which is equally important, and without which Medical Astrology cannot be understood. This factor consists of the four Elementary Qualities, Heat, Cold, Dryness and Moisture; which correspond with the four elements, Fire, Earth, Air and Water; with the four humours, Yellow Bile, Black Bile, Blood and Phlegm; and with many other things.

[1] A House has two meanings in Astrology. It may mean a twelfth part of the heavens, as will be shown presently, or it may mean a Sign of the Zodiac specifically appropriated to a particular Planet, which is its Lord.

Since there are twelve Signs of the Zodiac, Seven Planets, and twelve Houses of Heaven, it will be easily seen that the merely numerical combinations of any one of these with the others are indefinitely multitudinous; and when it is known that each may be combined with the others in many different ways, the complications become too great for the human intellect to follow; and since many of the combinations depend on considerations that are both vague and arbitrary, it is not surprising that scarcely any two Astrologers should combine them in the same way, or draw the same conclusions from the same disposition of the heavens.

Every Sign of the Zodiac, every Planet, and every House has certain special powers and influence, not only over mankind generally, but specially over individual men and women, according to the moment of their birth, according to their complexion, disposition and temperament, according to the place in which they live, and so forth; and in addition, every Sign, Planet, and House has special powers at certain times of life, and every Sign and Planet has its own elementary qualities, as hot and dry, cold and moist, and so forth, and has special power over some part of the body and some faculty of mind. Moreover, these powers, both general and special, are reinforced or diminished in so many ways that the memory can scarcely retain them; and since neither the reinforcement nor the diminution is susceptible of any exact computation, the result, even if all were to be allowed their proper weight, must always be dubious.

The Signs of the Zodiac.

These, of course, are twelve in number. In Astronomy they are disposed in the order in which the sun successively occupies them, Aries, Taurus and Gemini being the Signs of Spring; Cancer, Leo and Virgo those of Summer; Libra, Scorpio and Sagittarius those of Autumn; and Capricornus, Aquarius and Pisces the Signs of Winter. In Astrology, however, they are differently arranged, according to their several qualities or properties. They are still in groups of three, but each group forms, not a season of the year, but a Triplicity, thus:

Aries, the first month of Spring, Leo, the second month of Summer, and Sagittarius, the third month of Autumn, form the first Triplicity; every sign in which is hot and dry, regulates the Bilis flava, is masculine, diurnal, and is influential in youth. Its Lord is Sol by day and Jupiter by night.

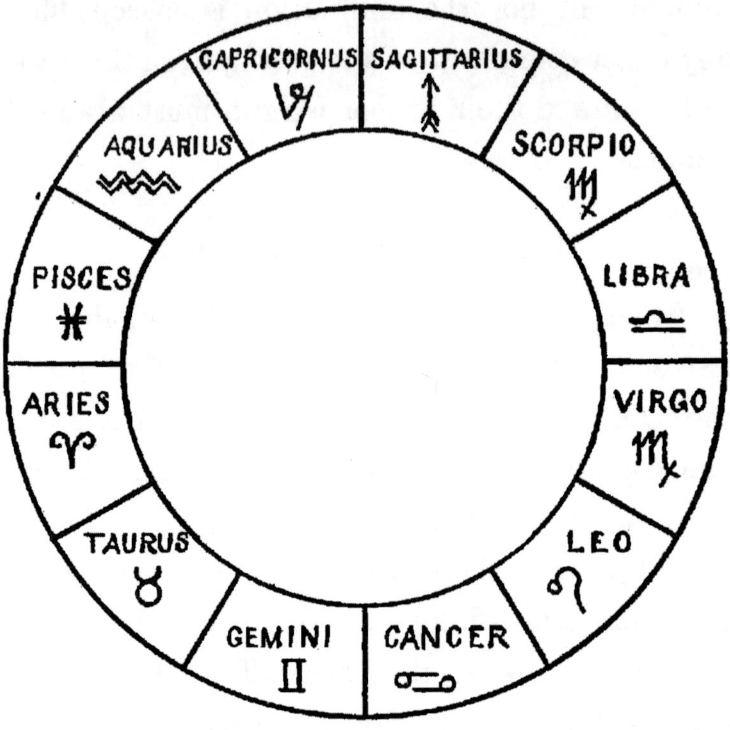

Fig. 1.

The second Triplicity consists of Taurus, the second Sign of Spring, Virgo, the third Sign of Summer, and Capricornus, the first of Winter. These Signs are cold and dry; their corresponding humour is Bilis atra; they are feminine, nocturnal, and preside over decrepitude. Their Lords are Venus by day and Luna by night.

The third Triplicity is composed of Gemini, Libra and Aquarius; the third of Spring, the first of Autumn, and the second of Winter. These are hot and moist in complexion, their humour is Sanguis, they are masculine and diurnal; they preside over our childhood, and their Lords are Saturn by day and Mercury by night.

The Signs of the fourth Triplicity are Cancer, the first of Summer, Scorpio, the second of Autumn, and Pisces, the third of Winter. They are cold and moist; their humour is Pituita; they are feminine and nocturnal; they regulate the middle period of life; and their Lords are Venus by day and Mars by night.

It is also important to know that some signs are mobile, such are Cancer, Libra, Capricornus and Pisces; others are stable, and such are Taurus, Leo, Scorpio and Aquarius; while a third group is mediocre with respect to mobility, as Aries, Gemini, Virgo and Sagittarius.

A masculine Sign is so called because a child conceived under the influence of that Sign will be a male; and children conceived under feminine

Signs are female. (Yet it is a fixed rule that all children are born under Aries, just as by the common law, all children born at sea are parishioners in Stepney.)

A Sign is diurnal or nocturnal according as its power is greater by day or by night.

In addition, every Sign has an aspect towards some particular part of the human body.

Aries is the principal and most important sign of all. In whatever scheme the Signs are reckoned, Aries comes first: consequently its aspect is to the head. Taurus relates to the neck and shoulders, because a bull is in these parts very robust. Gemini relates to the arms and hands, because the twins are represented as embracing, and the quality of embracing is in the arms and hands. Cancer pertains to the chest and the adjacent parts, because a crab is very robust in the chest and thereabouts. Leo pertains to the heart and the mouth of the stomach, because the whole virtue of a lion is in his courage. Virgo relates to the intestines, the base of the stomach and umbilicus, because the virtue of a virgin resides therein. Libra relates to the kidneys, because they lie equally balanced, one on each side of the spine. Scorpio refers to the genitals, because the whole virtue of the scorpion is in his tail, and these are the caudalia of man. The aspect of Sagittarius is to the hips, of Capricornus to the knees, of Aquarius to the legs, and of Pisces to the feet, these being the parts of the body, as those are the Signs, that come next in order.

The Planets.

It is scarcely necessary to remind this audience that in the time when Astrology came into being, the earth was the centre of the universe, and the Planets were seven in number, Uranus and Neptune being then as unknown as Pallas and Ceres, while the sun and moon differed from the other wandering stars only in their greater size and lustre, and in the greater regularity of their movements.

There was a certain conventional order, the origin of which cannot now be traced, in which the Planets were always enumerated; an order that does not correspond with their relative size and importance, for then the Sun would come first. It is Saturn, however, that takes precedence, and is followed by Jupiter, Mars, Sol, Venus, Mercury and Luna, in the order in which I have named them.

The range of influence of the Planets over matters terrestrial was plenary. On the whole, the term influence best conveys the meaning of the Astrological term 'aspect,' which is more than 'corresponds with,' a term that is sometimes substituted for 'aspect.' Though as to some things which they aspected, or with which they corresponded, such as the Zodiacal signs and the four elements, the Planets were neither productive nor regulative, yet with respect to most things, they were at least regulative, and as to many were actually originating. For instance, Guy de Chauliac, called by Fallopius the father of Surgery, as Hippocrates is the father of Medicine, attributed the great plague of 1345 to the conjunction of the three planets, Saturn, Jupiter and Mars, in Aquarius on March 24th of that year.

Torella, physician to Caesar Borgia and Pope Alexander VI, attributed syphilis to a peculiar conjunction of the Planets. So does Basil Valentinus, and so does Petrus Maynardus, who was able, moreover, to predict that it would come to an end in 1584. The College of Physicians of Paris attributed the Black Death of 1349 to a vapour or fog generated by the struggle between the constellations, which combated the rays of the sun and the warmth of the heavenly fire, struggling violently with the waters of the great sea. 'This vapour,' they said, 'will continue to spread as long as the sun is in Leo....We are of opinion that the constellations with the aid of nature strive by virtue of their divine might to protect and heal the human race.'

Taken together, the Planets had jurisdiction over everything, but not indiscriminately. Each Planet had its own peculiar jurisdiction over some things, while other Planets divided between them the jurisdiction over other things of that kind. Like the Signs of the Zodiac, each of the Planets had a jurisdiction over some part of the human body, but this was only a small region of its sway. Every Planet aspected its own element, and its own complexion, or pair of elementary qualities, so that Saturn, for instance, was cold and dry, Jupiter hot and moist, and so forth. Each Planet had its own colour, odour and taste; each its own groups of animals and plants; each its own metal, and we still speak of Saturnine poisoning, of crocus Martis, and of the metal Mercury; each has its own plants, its own day of the week and hour of the day; and what is more germane to the present purpose, every Planet had its corresponding humour, part of the body, sense, faculty, part of the mind, bodily configuration and mental temperament, its time of life, and its peculiar diseases and mode of death.

One or two instances will be enough to exemplify the way in which sublunary affairs are apportioned among the Planets. Take for instance animals: of these, Saturn has jurisdiction over the camel, the bear, the ass, the cat, the owl, the bat, the tortoise, the mouse, the beetle; and generally, over beasts of evil omen or of slow movement. The aspect of Jupiter is to the wise, the swift, and the strong: to the elephant, the stag and the bull. Mars aspects the horse, the wolf, the bee, the dog, the ostrich, venomous snakes, scorpions and spiders; all either fighters or noxious to human beings. Sol presides over regal and dominant animals, the lion, the eagle and the cock. Venus has jurisdiction over the goat, the sheep, the pheasant, the partridge, the pigeon, the dove and the sparrow; all amatory, and either polygamous or otherwise prolific. The aspect of Mercury is to the fox, the ape, the serpent, the parrot, the spider, the bee and the ant, and generally, to animals that are reputed wise or cunning. Luna influences the hare, the swan, the nightingale, the frog, fish, landsnails, crabs and shellfish, and generally, animals that are nocturnal or aquatic.

Of plants, Saturn has jurisdiction over the oak, the mespilus, the rue, the hellebore, and generally over those of slow growth, of narcotic virtue, and of crass substance. Jupiter over the laurel, the sandal-wood, the cinnamon, the balsam and the incense tree. Mars over pepper, ginger, mustard, jalap, scammony, colocynth, euphorbium, and generally over all bitter plants and hot poisons. Sol aspects the palm, rosemary, heliotrope, crocus, and all aromatics. Venus the olive, the pine, the lily, the rose and the pea; Mercury the corylus and the millefoil; and Luna the cucumber, the gourd, pepin fruits, *i.e.* apples and pears, and lettuce.

The minerals of Saturn are lead and all black stones; of Jupiter, tin, the sapphire, and the amethyst; of Mars, iron, jasper, and magnesia; of Sol, gold, carbuncles, and crysolite; of Venus, copper, smaragdus, turquoise, and coral; of Mercury, quicksilver, chalcedony, and cornelian; and of Luna, silver, crystals, beryl, and the diamond.

I defer to the next lecture the consideration of those planetary aspects that have a special bearing upon medicine, but this is perhaps the proper place to make the very important distinction between the benevolent, propitious, or fortunate Planets and those that are malevolent, unpropitious, or unlucky. The fortunate, or benevolent, or propitious Planets are Jupiter, Sol, and Venus, of which the first and last are lucky in the highest degree. Saturn, Mars, and Luna are malevolent, unpropitious, and unlucky. Mercury is variable in this respect. He has scarcely any character of his own, but he reinforces the benevolence or the malevolence, as the case may be, of whatever Planet may be in conjunction with him, or may be favourably aspected by him.

It is evident, if these premises are granted, that the course and termination of every malady in every sick person depend on the relative power, with respect to other Planets, of the particular Planet or Planets that have jurisdiction in the matter. They will depend, in the first place, on the Planet that has jurisdiction over the temperament, as Saturn if he is saturnine, Jupiter if he is jovial, Mars if he is martial, and so forth. They will depend also on the Planet that presides over the humour that is peccant, as yellow bile, black bile, blood or phlegm. They will depend on the Planet that governs the part of the body that is diseased; on that which governs the disease; on that which has jurisdiction at the time of life at which the sick person is arrived; on that which presided over his nativity, and so forth. Here are at least six circumstances to be taken into account, and of course, the Planet that governs one of these circumstances may not be the same, and in fact must be different from those which govern others. So that seven Planets may all be influencing the disease and the sick person at once, and may all be pulling in different directions, some towards health and some towards death, some towards acuteness and some towards chronicity of the disease. It is evident, therefore, that his fate must depend on the relative powers of the propitious and unpropitious Planets, and that it is of the utmost importance to determine the factors on which the powers of the Planets depend, and to estimate their strength in any particular case.

This is by no means easy, for the factors are very numerous. It will be enough to obtain an approximate estimate, however, if we confine our consideration to the ten in the following enumeration.

The power of a Planet at any given moment depends on:

1. The Sign of the Zodiac in which it is situated at that moment.
2. The Sign of which the Planet is Lord.
3. The Sign in which the Planet rejoices.
4. The Signs in which the Planet ascends or descends.
5. The House in which the Planet is situated.
6. The House in which the Planet rejoices.
7. The position or aspect of the Planet towards other Planets.
8. The aspect of the Planet to the Ascendent.
9. The motion of the Planet, as fast or slow, direct or retrograde.
10. The day and hour.

In this estimation of the powers of the Planets, much depends on the Houses of Heaven, and these must be described before we can proceed.

The Houses of Heaven.

We all recognise that, while the stars have an apparent motion from the eastern horizon up to the vertical meridian, and down again to the western horizon, yet the horizons and the vertical meridian keep their places with respect to us, and do not move. The eastern horizon and the vertical meridian enclose between them a fourth part of the heavens, whose content is continually changing, as the stars rise above the eastern horizon and reach and pass the meridian. Similarly, from the meridian to the western horizon is another fourth part; and the two remaining fourths are beneath the horizon, and are divided from one another by the inferior vertical meridian, all these fourth parts remaining stationary, while the stars occupy them each in turn in the daily revolution of the heavens. Now imagine each of these fixed quarters of heaven to be divided by three equidistant meridians: the heavens will then be divided into twelve parts, six above the horizon and six below, whose starry contents are continually changing. These twelve divisions are the twelve Houses of Heaven.

That is to say, they are so if the meridians which divide them meet at the north and south poles of the horizon of the place; and it was the usual rule in Astrology so to consider them; but it was not the invariable rule. Some astrologers put the meeting places at the celestial poles, and then the Houses were divided by the ordinary meridians. Others put the meeting places at the Zenith and the Nadir of the place. It is manifest that those astrologers who computed the positions of the Planets in one set of Houses, must arrive at very different results from those who computed the positions in another set; for a Planet might be in one House according to one computation, and in a different House according to another.

That House which is immediately below the eastern horizon, so that the stars therein are the next to rise above the horizon, is the first House, which is also called the Ascendent House, or shortly, the Ascendent. It is the principal House, the most powerful House, and takes rank over all the others. The Planet or Planets that occupy the Ascendent chiefly determine the fate of the native. The rest of the Houses are known by numbers, and follow one another widdershins, that is, in the order reverse to the movement of the hands of a clock. The second and third are between the Ascendent and the lower vertical meridian; the fourth, fifth and sixth between the lower vertical meridian and the western horizon; and so on until the twelfth house meets the first at the eastern horizon.

The anterior boundary of each House, the meridian which the stars in that House will cross next, is called the cusp of that House; and from the cusp the position of the Planets in the House is measured in degrees and minutes. The cusp of the Ascendent House is called the horoscope; and I may here correct a prevalent error with respect to this term. It is customary to speak of casting a horoscope, as if that were a possible and usual operation in Astrology. What is meant by the expression is casting a nativity or geniture; that is to say, setting out, on a plan of the Houses of Heaven, the position of the Signs of the Zodiac and of the Planets in the respective Houses that they occupied at the moment of birth. Similarly, we may cast a decumbiture, that is, we may set out a similar plan for the moment a disease begins; and such an operation was as necessary in the daily routine of a physician as is now the taking the temperature of the patient: but it is manifest that we cannot in this sense cast a horoscope, for the horoscope is but the cusp of the Ascendent.

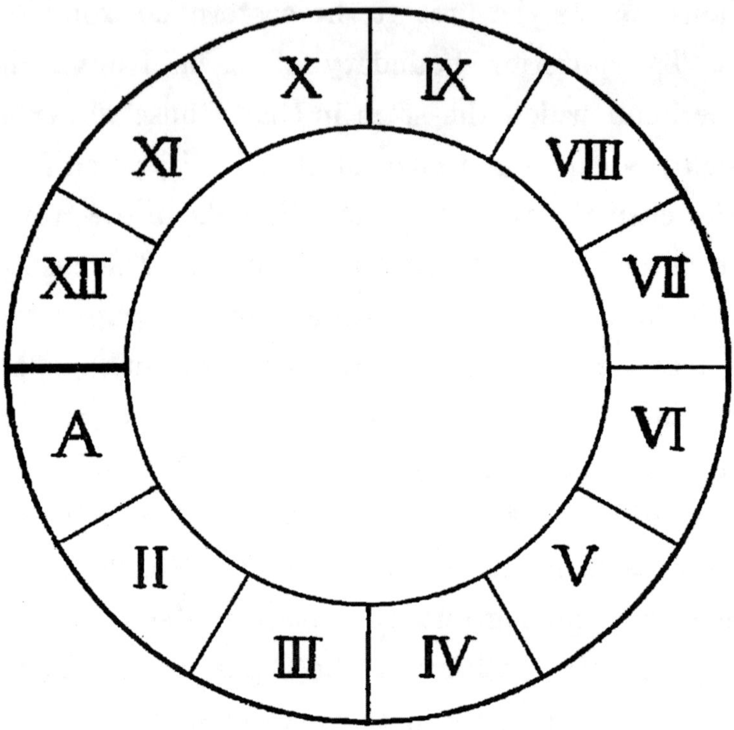

Fig. 2.

This is the most obvious method of setting out the Houses, but it was not usually adopted, perhaps because compasscs were not common, and circles not so easy to draw as straight lines. The conventional figure, on which the positions of the heavenly bodies were always set out, was thus:

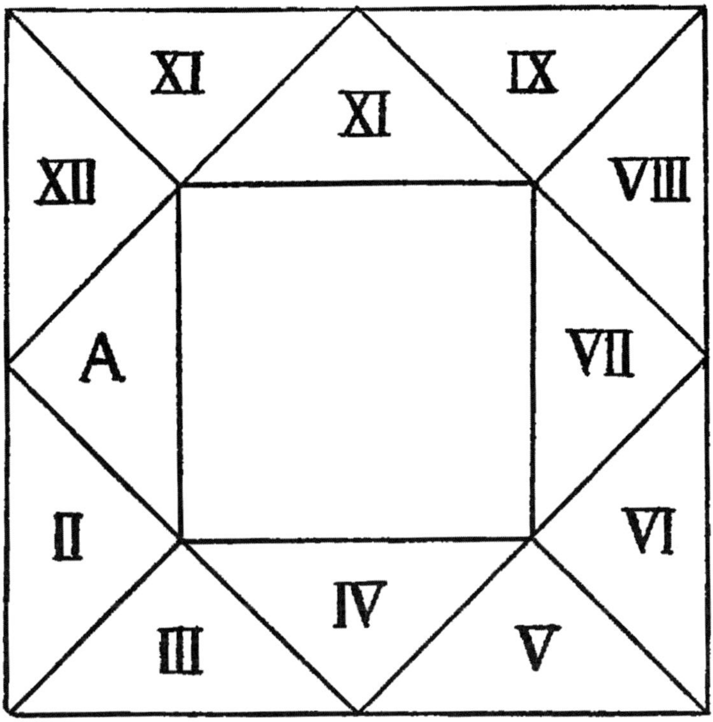

Fig. 3.

Each House of Heaven, like each Sign of the Zodiac and each Planet, has its special aspect, jurisdiction, or influence over human affairs; but unlike the Signs and the Planets, the Houses are not complexionate: they are neither hot nor cold, neither moist nor dry.

Just as Aries is the first, the most powerful and important of the Signs, and Luna the most powerful and important of the Planets, so the Ascendent is the most powerful and important of the Houses. When a Planet is in the Ascendent, its power is paramount over all the other Planets, wherever they may be; still, it may be strongly influenced by them. The Ascendent is the House of projects, of the beginnings of things, especially of journeys; it is the House of life, of movement, and of questions and answers.

The second House is the House of riches, and of servants; and signifies the end of youth, and the lessening of the years of life.

The third House is the House of brothers and sisters; of acquaintances and friends; of heirs; of changes; of continuance of journeys; of quiet of kingdoms; of religion, and ministers of religion.

The fourth House is the House of parents; of heredity; of towns in which the native lives, and in which he is born, and of his fate after death.

The fifth House is the House of children; of eating and drinking; of games; of fighting; of pictures, vessels and money.

The sixth House is the House of sickness and

health; of servants; of domestic animals; and of receiving.

The seventh House is the House of women; of marriage; of contentions and strife; of saints; and of thieves; and signifies the middle of life.

The eighth House is the House of Death; of fear; of riches; and of the last years of life.

The ninth House is of pilgrimages and journeys; of faith; of wisdom and philosophy; of books; of rumours; and of sleep.

The tenth House is the Royal House. It is the House of dignities; of laws; of princes and magistrates; of memories; of mothers; and of half of the years of life.

The eleventh House is the House of fortune; of good faith; of friends and allies.

The twelfth House is the House of unfriends, and of bad faith; of labour; of battles; of sadness; and of beasts and birds.

The strongest House of all is the Ascendent. Next to this are the other *angulares*, which immediately precede the other cardinal points, viz.—the fourth, seventh and tenth, all powerful and propitious Houses. The next in succession are called the successors of the *angulares*, and are less powerful than the *angulares,* but still disposed to be good, or propitious. The remaining Houses, the third, sixth, ninth and twelfth, are called *ab angulis cadentes,* and are unpropitious, and disposed to evil.

We are now in a position to discover the ways in which the power of a Planet is increased or diminished.

In the first place, every Planet is related to certain Signs of the Zodiac in three different ways. First, it has a Sign or Signs peculiar to itself, which are called the houses of the Planet, and of this house, or of these houses, the planet is Lord. Second, every Planet has a Sign in which it rejoices. When situated in any of these Signs, and especially when in its house, the power of the Planet is augmented. Third, every Planet is exalted in a certain Sign, and depressed in that which is diametrically opposite, and the power of the Planet is increased or diminished according as the one or the other of these Signs is in the Ascendent.

For instance, Saturn is Lord of Capricorn essentially, and of Aquarius accidentally; he rejoices in Aquarius, is exalted in Libra, and depressed in Aries. Consequently, his power is at its maximum when he is in Capricorn, and is augmented when he is in Aquarius. It is increased when Libra is in the Ascendent, and subdued when Aries is in that House. Saturn (chronos) regulates the beginnings of things, especially of things relating to the earth, such as planting, sowing, ploughing, and other operations of agriculture. Such operations ought therefore to be begun when Saturn has power, as when he is in the Ascendent, or in Capricorn or Aquarius, provided that Aries is not in the Ascendent. If Libra should be in the Ascendent, however, such operations can scarcely fail to be successful.

A hot Planet in a hot Sign will have its heat augmented; but in a cold Sign its heat will be reduced; and so of the other elementary qualities. A moist Planet in a humid Sign will be dripping wet, and will aggravate diseases due to moisture.

We have seen that certain Houses are more propitious than others, those, namely, whose cusp is on the horizon or on one of the vertical meridians. A benevolent Planet will be doubly so when in a propitious House, but will have little power to benefit when it is in an unpropitious House.

The House in which it is situated influences a Planet in more ways than this. Every Planet has not only a Sign, but a House also in which it rejoices; and when it is in this House its power is augmented. Mercury rejoices in the Ascendent, Luna in the third House, Mars in the sixth, Sol in the ninth, Jupiter in the eleventh, and Saturn in the twelfth.

Perhaps the most important factor in modifying the power of the Planets, and certainly the factor to which the most importance is attached, is their relative position or aspect with respect to one another, and to the Ascendent.

The first aspect of Planets to one another is Conjunction, which, like other terms in Astrology, and in its congener, Logic, is not always used in the same sense. Planets are said by some authorities to be in conjunction when they are within 2° of one another; by others, when they are within 15° of each other; by others, when they are in the same Sign, and by others when they are in the same House. All are agreed, however, that whenever a Planet is within 15° of Sol, it is combust, and its powers are for the time abolished. Otherwise, when Planets of the same qualities are in conjunction, they corroborate and reinforce one another; but when Planets of opposing qualities are in conjunction, each cancels a part of the power of the other; so that when a good Planet is conjoined with an evil one, the malice of this is tempered, and the benevolence of that is debilitated. One of my authorities, Arnaldus de Villanova, gives the following instance. 'When you are anxious to begin some good work, you should see that Luna makes junction with benevolent Planets, or at any rate, is well separated from bad ones; but he who wants to do evil, as for example, to poison a little girl, or anything of that kind, ought to choose a time when Luna is conjoined with bad, or is separated from good Planets.'

The second aspect is Sextile. This is when two Planets are separated by a sixth part of the Zodiac, or by two Signs. Such an aspect is moderately friendly—not manifestly, but occultly, or of hidden benevolence.

The third aspect is Quartile, and is when a Planet aspects another through three Signs, which is a fourth part of the Zodiac. Such an aspect is of moderate or occult unfriendliness or conflict.

The fourth aspect is Trine, when a Planet aspects another from a distance of four Signs, or a third part of the Zodiac. This is the aspect of warm friendship, and perfect benevolence.

The last aspect is Opposition, when one Planet is distant from another by half the Signs of the Zodiac. This is the most hostile aspect of all; it is the aspect of open unfriendliness, hatred, and perdition.

Every Planet has two movements. First, it partakes of the general movement of the heavenly bodies, rising in the East and setting in the West, a movement due to the *primum mobile*; and second, it has its own proper motion among the stars, which varies in rapidity, and is sometimes direct, sometimes retrograde, and sometimes a-bolished, so that the Planet is stationary among the stars. The speed of this proper motion varies greatly, Luna completing her course in 28 days, or thereabouts, and Saturn requiring 29 years. The motion of the Planets is of much importance in medicine, for acute diseases, whose course is rapid, are governed by the moon, whose motion is rapid, while chronic diseases, whose course is slow, are governed by the sun, whose course is likewise slow. If any Planet that is regulating the course of a disease should become retrograde in its motion, the patient will of course get worse.

Lastly, every Planet has its hour, in which it is dominant; and, subject to the dominance of the Planet that rules the hour, every Planet dominates that day of the week of which its hour is the first. Thus, Saturn dominates completely the first hour of Saturday, and in a less degree, and subject to the influence of the other Planets, the whole of the *dies Sabbathum.* Jupiter rules the second hour of Saturday, Mars the third, and so on until Luna dominates the seventh hour, and then Saturn again takes up the tale, and rules the eighth. The rotation is then continued, so that Saturn comes in again at the fifteenth and twenty-second hours; Jupiter follows at the twenty-third; Mars at the twenty-fourth, which completes the day. The next Planet on the rota is Sol, which therefore takes the first hour, and in less degree the whole, of the following day, which is accordingly *Dies Solis,* or Sunday.

It is scarcely necessary to point out that every undertaking to which any given Planet is propitious ought to be begun in the hour in which that Planet is dominant, and if possible on his day. So all operations of husbandry should be begun on Saturday, or if on any other day, then in the hour of Saturn. When written directions are given as to any undertaking, the Planet that is propitious to that undertaking should be signified, so that the undertaking, whatever it may be, may be begun in the hour of that Planet. If we give written directions for sowing seed, or planting, or any of the operations of husbandry, we should preface our directions with the sign of Saturn. If we write to a commercial correspondent instructions to buy or sell, we should remind him of the hour and day propitious to the transaction by placing at the head of our instructions the sign of the Planet Mercury. Now, the Planet that is most propitious to the operation of letting blood, and to taking medicine, is Jupiter, and therefore all written directions for letting blood or administering medicine should bear the sign of Jupiter; and the sign of Jupiter is ♃ = ℞, which still heads all our prescriptions, and testifies to the intimate connexion that existed aforetime between Astrology and Medicine.

If we keep at our fingers' ends the knowledge we have now gained of the rudiments of Astrological lore, we shall be in a position to turn that knowledge to practical use, to erect a scheme of the heavens at the nativity of any given person, and to interpret that scheme so as to predict at least the general course of his life, and, if we have sufficient skill, the individual incidents therein. For this purpose it is convenient to select a person whose career is closed, because this gives us the double advantage of ascertaining whether our predictions are correct, and of keeping an eye on his career during the course of our interpretations, so that they may not go too wide of the mark. I select therefore a distinguished man, Charles XII of Sweden, whose career is familiar to you all.

As is usual, the pole of the Houses is at the horizontal north of the place, Stockholm, and not at the celestial pole, and therefore the latitude is given, and the Houses do not correspond with the Signs of the Zodiac. Taurus, for instance, occupies the whole of the fifth House, with six degrees of the fourth, and twenty of the sixth; while Aquarius lies wholly within the second, which includes also seven degrees of Capricorn and five of Pisces.

The first omen that attracts our attention is that Mars, the military planet, occupies the twelfth

House, the House of battles and of enemies. We predict, therefore, that

> No joys to him pacific scepters yield,
> War sounds the trump, he rushes to the field;
>
> . . . .
>
> Peace courts his hand, but spreads her charms in vain;
> 'Think nothing gain'd,' he cries, 'till nought remain!'

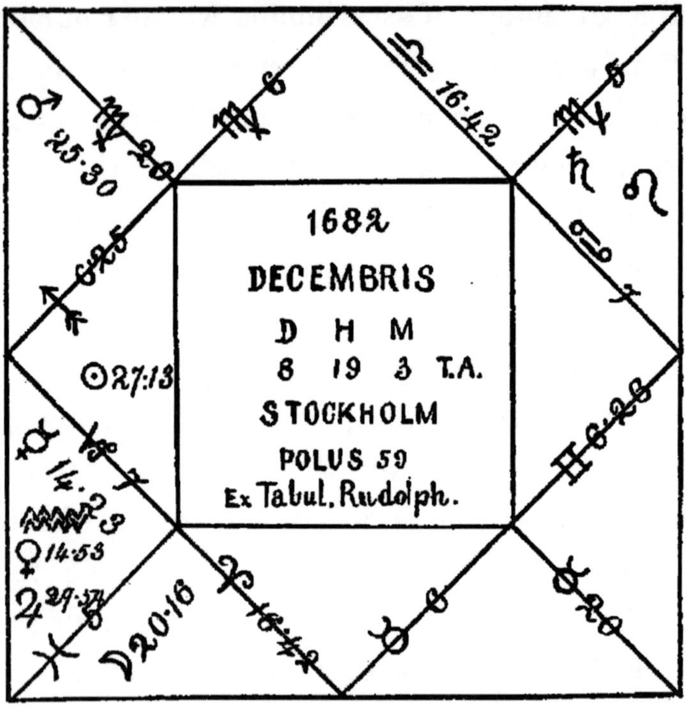

Fig. 4. Nativitas Caroli Duodecimi, Regis Sueciæ.

Venus, in the second House, does not aspect the native, and exerts no influence over him; and Charles XII was notoriously insusceptible to the charms of love. He was a neglecter and despiser of women—

> O'er love, o'er fear extends his wide domain,
> Unconquer'd lord of pleasure and of pain.

Sol, in the Ascendent, predicts for the native an illustrious and glorious career, and equips him with the necessary qualities—

> A frame of adamant, a soul of fire,
> No dangers fright him, and no labours tire;
> . . . .
> Behold surrounding kings their pow'r combine,
> And one capitulate, and one resign.

But Mars is an unpropitious Planet, a Planet of ill omen, and his presence in the House of battles cannot but signify military disaster: Luna, in sextile to the Ascendent, exerts an evil influence, which Jupiter, sequestered in the second House from exerting any counteracting sway, is powerless to restrain. What is the inevitable consequence?—

> He comes, not want nor cold his course delay;—
> Hide, blushing Glory, hide Pultowa's day:
> The vanquish'd hero leaves his brok'n bands,
> And shews his miseries in distant lands;
> Condemn'd a needy supplicant to wait,
> While ladies interpose, and slaves debate.

Finally, Saturn, a very malevolent Planet, is most ominously situated in the eighth House, the House of Death, a certain indication that death will come early and in disastrous circumstances. How true the indication let the poet testify:

> But did not Chance at length her error mend?
> Did no subverted empire mark his end?
> Did rival monarchs give the fatal wound?
> Or hostile millions press him to the ground?
> His fall was destin'd to a barren strand,
> A petty fortress, and a dubious hand;
> He left a name, at which the world grew pale,
> To point a moral, or adorn a tale.

LECTURE II

HAVING discovered in the last Lecture the general principles of Astrology, we are now in a position to discuss their application to medicine. We have already found that every Zodiacal Sign and every Planet has its own complexion, or pair of elementary qualities, as hot and dry, hot and moist, cold and dry, or cold and moist, and that each has, accordingly, power over the corresponding humour—yellow bile, blood, black bile or phlegm. We must now remark that among the powers of the Signs and the Planets are some, specially appertaining to medicine, that were omitted in the previous review.

Each Planet has its own peculiar power over the developing fœtus, and exercises this power at a certain period of pregnancy. Saturn has power in the first month after conception, and by its own frigidity (Saturn being cold and dry) infrigidates the fœtus, coagulates it, and drys it up, so causing early abortions. Jupiter is potent in the second month, and bestows on the embryo the *spiritus naturalis.* Mars, in the third month, supplies the concept with bones, and generally composes, or, as we should say, differentiates, the various internal organs. Sol, in the fourth month, supplies the concept with blood, and perfects the heart and liver. Venus, in the fifth month, gives to the concept ears, eyebrows and pudenda. Mercury, in the sixth month, opens the nose and mouth ; and Luna, in the seventh month, causes the development of the lungs, and divides the fingers and toes according to their places.

After birth, each Planet takes under its jurisdiction certain organs and tissues of the body, and certain faculties of the mind ; and has, moreover, jurisdiction over certain diseases and certain modes of death.

Saturn, which is cold and dry, and therefore regulates the black bile, presides also over the bones, teeth, cartilages, the right ear, the spleen and the bladder ; and over the memory. It has power, of course, over the diseases of these parts, and in addition, over quartan fever, scabies, lepra, tabes, melancholia, paralysis, icterus niger, dropsy, cancer, cough, asthma, phthisis, deafness of the right ear, and hernia. Under Saturn occur sudden and violent deaths by falls, precipitation, shipwreck, suffocation, hanging, lead-poisoning, and death at the hands of the public executioner.

Jupiter has jurisdiction over the radical moisture, over the blood, the liver, the pulmonary veins, the diaphragm, and the muscles of the trunk ; over the senses of touch and smell ; over the judgment, and the *appetitus concupiscibilis* ; over the diseases of these parts and faculties, and in addition over small-pox, angina, inflammation, pleurisies and peripneumonias. Deaths due to the influence of Jupiter occur in war, in duels, and by the command of Princes.

Mars has power over the yellow bile, the gall-bladder, the left ear, the pudenda and the kidneys. He prompts the *appetitus irascibilis.* The diseases due to his influence are acute fevers, plague, yellow jaundice, convulsions, hæmorrhages, carbuncles, erysipelas, ulcers, and phagedæna. He causes death by weapons of steel, from fire, from projectiles, by beheading, mutilation, bites of animals, especially venomous animals, by the slaughters and blood-letting of ignorant surgeons, and death from burns.

Sol regulates the heart, the arteries, the right eye, the right side in men and the left side in women; the vital spirits and the bilious blood; the sight of the right eye in men, and of the left in women, and all good desires. The diseases due to the influence of the sun are ephemeral fevers, syncope, spasm, catarrhs, and diseases of the eyes. When Sol causes death, it is by plague, by syncope, or on the field of battle.

Venus presides over the pituitous blood and semen: over the throat, the breasts, the abdomen, the uterus and genitalia; over taste and smell, touch and the pleasurable sensations, and the *appetitus concupiscibilis.* The diseases due to Venus are lues venerea, gonorrhœa, priapism, barrenness from cold and moisture (Venus being cold and moist), lientery, and abscesses. Deaths due to her influence are those from poison and from sexual excess.

Mercury has jurisdiction over the animal spirits, over the legs and feet, the hands and fingers, the tongue, the nerves, and the ligaments; over taste and hearing, common sense, imagination and reason. The diseases that he influences are erratic and relapsing fevers, mania, phrenitis, deliria, insanity, epilepsy, convulsion, balbuties, and cough with profuse expectoration. Under his influence occur deaths by poison, by witchcraft, and by process of law for perjury, forgery, and false money.

Finally, Luna presides over the phlegm, the brain, the left eye, the right side in women and the left in men, the stomach, and the membranes; over the sight of the right eye in women and of the left in men; over fear; over quotidian fevers, epilepsy, apoplexy, fatuity, vomiting, fluxes, such as diarrhoea and menorrhagia, dropsy, and cold abscesses. She brings those deaths that occur from superpurgation and from drowning.

It would seem, from the several jurisdictions here assigned to Mercury and Luna, that those whom we call lunatics ought properly to be called Mercurials, for though the moon rules the brain, Mercury has jurisdiction, as we have seen, over mania, phrenitis, delirium, and insanity; and, strictly speaking, no one with any of these maladies ought to be called a lunatic. Lunacy in the strict sense is fatuity interrupted by lucid intervals, as we shall find further on, and this is the sense that it had in law down to the passing of the Lunacy Acts. Until these enactments, the legal meaning of a lunatic was a fatuous or demented person who had, nevertheless, intervals of lucidity; and though in common speech the meaning became generalised, and the term was used to include all insane persons, whatever the nature of their insanity, and whether it was interrupted or continuous, yet lawyers, who are always both more precise and more conservative in the application of terms than other men, continued to use the term lunacy in its strict sense till the middle of the last century.

With respect to the corporature, or the bodily configuration, which, with the corresponding mental disposition, is aspected by the several Planets, there is much misapprehension; and the true doctrine is corrupted, and attenuated to a mere remnant. We are apt to consider that a Saturnine person is taciturn, cynical, and disposed to be malevolent; that a Jovial person is good-humoured and hilarious; that a Mercurial person is restless and vagrant, not continuing in one stay; that a Martial person has a soldierly bearing; and that a Lunatic is out of his mind; and although we should not be wrong in attributing these mental dispositions to the persons so denominated, we should give them but a tithe of the mental qualities the names actually connote; and we have forgotten altogether, not only that there is a corporature, or bodily configuration, that accompanies and indicates each mental temperament, but also that there are persons of Solar and Venereal temperament as well as those that are Jovial, Saturnine, and so forth. The corporature, and the mental disposition that accompanies and is signified by it, are precise and detailed, so that the expert astrologer can tell at a glance what sort of person he has to deal with, and what Planet has jurisdiction over that person's life, fortunes, and health.

Those, for instance, who are Saturnine, may be known by the following physical signs: they are moderately fleshy, of medium height, their countenances are long, their eyes large and black, their teeth very large; they are of dark complexion, have scanty straight black hair, thin beards, are pigeon-toed, and of truculent bearing. When well affected by the Planet, persons of such a corporature are profound thinkers, investigators of mysteries, prudent, reticent, inclined to solitude, suspicious, laborious, patient, persevering, lovers of work, eager for gain, and masterful. When ill affected by the Planet, they are sad, melancholy, austere, timid, miserly, querulous, taciturn, solitary, followers of the Black Art, suspicious, untruthful, malevolent, untrustworthy to the point of fraudulence, treacherous, and often suffer the penalties of the law for their misdeeds.

The favoured of Jupiter are, in configuration, fleshy, with rounded knees; they are of medium stature, elegant and majestic in bearing. In complexion they are rosy; their eyes are dark and rather large. They are prone to baldness, and have thick reddish beards. When well affected by the Planet, such persons are simple, just, pious, religious, faithful, humane, merciful, hilarious, gracious, open, affable, liberal, splendid, magnanimous and law-abiding. When ill affected, they have these qualities in excess. They are superstitious, sentimental, humanitarian, prodigal and vain-glorious.

The subjects of Mars are thin and well-proportioned; they are pale, with blue eyes and abundant curly hair, not only on the head but on the body. They are of middle stature, with large heads, round faces, small eyes, large nostrils, long teeth and military bearing. When well affected, they are strong, robust, brave, greedy of fame, irascible, given to hunting and games, vindictive, impatient of control, domineering, delighting in war and battles, contemptuous of danger, agile, ready, hasty, self-confident, and indifferent to religion. When ill affected, they are impious, unjust, arrogant, merciless, seditious, foolhardy, quarrelsome, brawlers, homicides, tyrants, incendiaries, robbers, thieves and bandits.

Those under the jurisdiction of Luna are tall, pale, good-looking, with light hair and eyes, and with becoming beards. When well affected, they are ingenious, subtle, sincere, open, honest and well-mannered; when ill affected, they are stupid even to fatuity, timid and restless. It is very important to know that, as might be expected, it is when the moon is waxing that they are well affected, and they are ill affected when she is on the wane. Here we see the origin of the legal doctrine, already alluded to, that a lunatic is a demented person who has lucid intervals, these intervals being when the moon is in the first two of her phases, while the periods of fatuity are the last two phases, when she is past the full, and her light is waning.

The votaries of Mercury are characterised by medium stature, a well-proportioned body, pleasing complexion, and yellow hair. They are graceful, with very small hands, feet and teeth; they have scanty beards, thin voices, and are rapid in their movements. When well affected, they are witty, studious, quick to learn, even without being taught; they are disputatious, wise, cautious, prudent, easily accommodating themselves to persons and circumstances; sociable and inquisitive. When ill affected, they are unstable, forgetful, apt to have hallucinations and to talk nonsense, liars, parasites, flatterers, deceitful, perfidious, perjurers, calumniators, forgers of wills, coiners of false money, meddlers in things that do not concern them, and dangerous counsellors.

Under the jurisdiction of Venus are those of medium stature, succulent, with delicate and fair complexions, good-looking, with crisp brown or blackish hair, dark eyes, narrow eyebrows, narrow chests, and thick thighs. When well affected, they are indolent, bland, pious, religious, merciful, peaceful, sociable, lovers of the arts of singing and of music, elegant and graceful, and given to delicacies and pleasures. They are lucky in love and in friendship, forgiving, and impatient under misfortune. When ill affected, they are timid, imprudent, effeminate, lecherous, and betrayers of women.

Lastly, the characters of those who are ruled by the Sun are a large head, a round and glowing face, large eyes, long hair which at length falls out and leaves them bald, and a sallow complexion. When well affected, they are pious, just, upright, faithful, open, chaste, worldly-wise, apt to anger, but magnanimous, honourable, splendid and magnificent, warm in friendship, and lovers of their wives and children.

It will have been noticed that the descriptions of the bodily configurations are not very definite, and we are warned by Maninius to be very careful of judging of the dominant Planet by the configuration of the body. This, he says, is a part of the science in which many fail; and it is not yet fully ascertained. The knowledge is to be attained by long experience only. Maninius had, indeed, good reason to inculcate caution in interpreting the indications obtained from Astrological lore, for he sought to clench the arguments with which he was defending Astrology from the attacks of

Gassendi, by predicting the death of the sceptic upon a certain date. When the date came round in due course, Gassendi unexpectedly refused to die, and Maninius then discovered a mistake in his calculation which had led him to antedate the event. He corrected the error, revised his prediction, and fixed another and later date, beyond which Gassendi could not survive. He seems, however, to have overlooked a second time some material factor, for his opponent lived on, and laughed him to scorn, giving much occasion to the enemy to blaspheme. Maninius, unfortunately, lacked the resource of Dean Swift, who was confronted with the same difficulty by the survival of the astrologer Partridge. Swift, under the pseudonym of Isaac Bickerstaff, predicted that Partridge would die "on the twenty-ninth of March next, about eleven at night, of a raging fever"; and, when the date was past, published a circumstantial account of the death, with a confession by Partridge of the imposture of his predictions. In vain Partridge denied the facts, for Bickerstaff gave five conclusive reasons for disbelieving these protestations, and for holding that Partridge was in fact dead, and in denying the fact had carried beyond the grave his proclivity for telling lies.

When it is remembered that any Sign of the Zodiac may be in any of the Houses of Heaven; that any Planet may be in any House, and may have any aspect, sextile, quartile, trine, or opposition, towards the Ascendent and towards the other Planets; and that the various Planets have by these means their powers reinforced or attenuated in the most various degrees; and when we remember further the different powers that different Planets have over different persons and different diseases, it will easily be seen that the variations are virtually infinite, and the whole scheme far too complicated to put to practical application.

In practice, however, the calculations of the physician were narrowed down to a small number of factors. Arnaldus de Villanova, a physician of great repute in the thirteenth century, limits these as follows:—A perfect physician, he says, should constantly bear in mind eight Astrological factors; and then we are disappointed to find that he enumerates only seven. It is no doubt the want of the eighth factor that has falsified the predictions that I have ventured to make in accordance with his rules. Be that as it may, the factors that he enumerates, as necessary for the perfect physician to consider, are these :

1. The thing concerning which the inquiry is made.
2. The Sign that is in the Ascendent.
3. The Lord of it. (Whether of the Sign or of the Ascendent is not clear.)
4. The Sign that is in the House of the thing inquired about. (In the case of sickness, this may be either the first House, the House of Life ; or the eighth, the House of Death ; or the sixth, the House of Diseases.)
5. The Lord of it. (Again, whether of the Sign or of the House is not clear.)
6. Its (?) relation to the Ascendent.
7. Its relation to the Moon.

These are to be interpreted in the following manner :

1. The Ascendent and the Lord of it signify the sick man.
2. The middle of Heaven (the tenth House) signifies his physician.

3. The sixth House and the Lord of it signify his disease.
4. The fourth House and the Lord of it signify his physic.

The consequences are these :

If there is evil in the Ascendent, or if the Lord of the Ascendent is subject to adverse influences, the patient will do badly ; but if these are propitious, he will do well.

If there should be a benevolent or propitious Lord of the tenth House, which signifies the physician, then his treatment will do the patient good ; but if the Lord should be evil, then the patient will be injured by the treatment.

If there should be a powerful influence for good in the eighth House, which is the House of Death, the patient will be quickly cured ; but if there should be an evil influence in this House, he will go from bad to worse.

Similarly, if there is good fortune in the fourth House, which is the House of Remedies, his medicine will do him good, but if evil fortune, the medicine will make him worse.

If the Sign in the Ascendent should be mobile, and Luna should be in a mobile Sign, such as Aries,

Cancer, Libra, or Capricorn, and the Lord of the Ascendent should also be in a mobile Sign, the illness will soon terminate, either well or badly, especially if Luna is in swift motion. If, however, it happens contrarily, it signifies a long illness, especially if Luna is in a stable Sign, as Taurus, Leo, Scorpio or Aquarius.

If the Lord of the Ascendent should be propitious, and free from adverse influences of other Planets, and Luna likewise, the illness will end favourably, especially if Luna and the Lord of the Ascendent should aspect favourably the Lord of the eighth House, which is the House of Death—that is, if they should be in sextile, and especially if they should be in trine, to that House.

But if Luna, or the Lord of the Ascendent, or the Lord of the House of Sickness, which is the sixth, should be combust and retrograde, or if the Lord of the Ascendent should be in the House of Death in conjunction with Mars or Saturn, both of them malevolent Planets, then there is no hope.

Also, if the moon should be in conjunction with a propitious Planet in the Ascendent, and should be moving forward and her light waxing, and both should be free from adverse influences, then the disease will be quickly cured; but if the moon should be in the House of Death, the patient cannot be saved.

And generally, whenever Luna and the Lord of the Ascendent are subject to adverse influences, it is a mortal sign, and we must fear death, or relapse, or long illness; but when they are fortunately situated, and aspected by well-disposed powers, as when Luna and the Lord are in the Ascendent, then it is a good sign, and *ad vitam.*

But if the House of Death, and the Lord of the House of Infirmity, or the Lord of the House of Death, are fortified by situation or by aspect, especially when they aspect the moon adversely, then it is a bad sign, and *ad mortem*; but when they are impeded or weakened, it is a good sign.

Now the position of the heavenly bodies in the Houses of Heaven alters from hour to hour, and a fatal disposition of them now may alter to a favourable one in a couple of hours, and *vice versâ.* Luna, which is now in the Ascendent, and therefore smiles upon the patient, will, in fourteen or fifteen hours' time, be in the eighth House, and condemn him to death. It is manifestly of the utmost importance, therefore, to fix upon the correct hour and minute for setting up the *tabula cœlestiarum*. It is to be feared, however, that in this matter astrological physicians allowed themselves a good deal of latitude. There are two fixed moments, one or other of which should be taken as that on which the scheme should be erected. One of these is the moment of birth; the other is the decumbiture.

It will be seen that the scheme of the nativity of Charles XII sets forth the year, the month, the day, hour, and minute of birth, and the scheme is erected accordingly, and admits of no doubt or variation. There was, however, a process known to Astrologers by the name of Rectification of the Nativity, a process the rules of which are difficult to discover, but the practical result was to shift the heavenly bodies from positions that were inconvenient to the Astrologer to positions more suitable to his purpose. I should never myself make an alteration of this nature, which does not seem to me quite justifiable, but, emboldened by this established astrological practice, I have ventured to make a trifling alteration in the scheme of nativity that I have placed before you as that of Charles XII. As originally erected, it referred not to the year 1682 but to the year 1594, and to the moment of birth, not of Charles XII, but of a previous King of Sweden, namely, Gustavus Adolphus, the Lion of the North, and the Bulwark of the Protestant Faith. In working it out, I found that by no ingenuity and by no artifice could I make the predictions to be drawn from this scheme of nativity fit in with the known career of that great and successful commander. They suited, however, with such surprising accuracy and appropriateness the career of his successor Charles XII that I felt it was a pity to allow myself to be fettered, in applying them to him, by a punctilio of needless scrupulosity. I did not venture to take that liberty with the facts that astrologers were accustomed to take, by altering the positions of the heavenly bodies in the Houses of Heaven; I merely altered the date by less than a century, and substituted the name of one King of Sweden for another.

In estimating the scheme of the heavens relating to the illness of a patient, it is always advisable to compare it with the scheme of his nativity. If that Planet which was Lord of the Ascendent in the nativity is favourably placed and fortunately aspected in the scheme of the decumbiture, and is neither combust nor retrograde, the patient will be strengthened and live, and *vice versâ.*

These are the considerations that should weigh with a perfect physician; but the authority I am now quoting from lived seven centuries ago, and the world was very different then from what it is now. It would appear that in those remote and benighted times there actually were physicians who were not perfect, and to temper the difficulties of astrological practice to these weaker brethren, they were taught a method of procedure that is shorter and easier, but less accurate. It will have been noticed how prominent a place is assigned to the moon in the explanations that have been given, although in setting up the scheme no separate mention was made of her, but she was just lumped in together with the other Planets, which had presumably equal value, except in as far as their power was subdued or enhanced by their position. In the modified and abbreviated scheme that was drawn up for the guidance of the general practitioner, the whole burden lay upon the moon. It was recognised that a busy practitioner could not be expected to have the correct positions of the Planets always at his fingers' ends; but he could scarcely be ignorant of the phase in which the moon was, of whether she was waxing or waning, or even of the Sign she occupied. Consequently, except to the very expert—to the dwellers in the Harley Street and Wimpole Street of that day—the moon alone was the guide to treatment and prognosis.

I must now go back for a moment, and call your attention to certain *Facultates Naturales* possessed by the human body, and governed by the Planets. These are the Retentrix, the Coctrix, the Expultrix, the Attractrix, the Vegatatrix and the Generatrix; and each has, of course, its corresponding complexion. Retention, for instance, is favoured by cold and drought, Digestion by heat and moisture, Expulsion by cold and moisture, and Attraction by heat and drought.

It follows, of course, that retentive medicines, given to check fluxes of any kind, should be administered either when Luna is in a sign that is cold and dry, such as Taurus, Virgo or Capricorn, or when one of these signs is in the Ascendent; and at such times retentive drugs should be not only administered but prepared, for their virtues are not in themselves, but are part of the celestial virtue communicated from the celestial bodies, from which all virtues are derived. So that retentive medicines, such as sugar of roses, diaciton and diapapaver, should be prepared as well as administered when one of these cold and dry signs is in the Ascendent, or when the moon is in one of them. If, however, we wish to reinforce the expulsive faculty, as for instance in constipation or amenorrhœa, the medicament must be prepared and administered when Luna is in Cancer, Scorpio or Pisces, or when one of them is in the Ascendent; for these Signs are cold and moist. In this case we must be careful, however; for if a purgative is given when the motion of Luna is retrograde, the expulsion will be retrograde, and instead of purgation we shall cause vomiting; but if we are so incautious and ignorant as to give purgatives when the moon is retrograde in Leo, which has an aspect to the heart and blood, we shall produce vomiting of blood.

Diseases of plethora are very dangerous when a man is taken sick upon a full moon, and diseases of wasting are most dangerous when he is taken sick upon a waning moon. Let me entreat you therefore to give physic for inanition when the moon is near the full, and for plethora when she has lost her light; and remember that a humour can scarcely be diminished but when the moon is waning, nor increased except when she is waxing.

It is very bad when, in the beginning of a sickness, the moon is in a Sign of the nature of the peccant humour, as in the hot and dry Signs Aries, Leo or Sagittarius, when the peccant humour is choler; the cold and dry Signs Taurus, Capricorn or Virgo, when it is melancholy; the hot and moist Signs Gemini, Libra or Aquarius, when it is blood; or the cold and moist signs Cancer, Scorpio or Pisces, when it is phlegm.

Naturally, when she is in a fiery Sign, it is easy to amend a disease of phlegm, but if choler abound, wait until she is in a watery Sign.

We see, therefore, how very important it is to consider the aspect of the heavens before we begin our treatment; and though it is true that patients do sometimes recover under the care of ignorant physicians who take no account of these things, yet in such cases, says my authority, the patient recovers by accident, and not by the skill of the physician.

An additional reason for studying the motion of the moon in illness is because this motion regulates the critical days. A crisis is defined as a swift and vehement motion of a disease, leading to recovery or death. Strictly speaking, those only are true crises which lead to recovery, but inaccuracy and corruption have crept into the meaning, until some authors enumerate six kinds of crisis, which I need not enumerate here; but all authorities are agreed, and their agreement seems to me to arise from everyone copying the words of his predecessor, that for a true and perfect crisis six conditions must be fulfilled.

In the first place, the crisis must be complete, that is to say, the whole of the *materia peccans* must be evacuated; for instance, all the bile in tertian fever, and all the phlegm in quotidian fever. If the whole of the *materia peccans* is not evacuated, it is evident that the patient may relapse.

The second condition is that none of the peccant material should remain. This is evidently quite as important as the first, that all of it should be evacuated.

The third condition is that health must be completely regained, and there must be no terrible accidents or pernecabilibus, such as running of the eyes.

The fourth condition is that the crisis must be manifest; that is to say, there must be a sensible evacuation of the *materia peccans.*

The fifth condition is that the crisis must make indication, and as to the meaning of this, I have come, after long and careful study, to the conclusions on another subject arrived at by my authority, and piously expressed by him in the words, *Deus solus cognoscit, quia habet neque caput neque caudam.*

The sixth condition is that the crisis must occur on a critical day.

The critical days are governed entirely by the motion and positions of the moon. It is clear that there can be no crisis for good except *materiâ peccante coctâ,* and it is evident that the *materia peccans* cannot be digested in as short a time as two days; consequently the first and second days of a disease cannot be critical. The third day is intercadent, and the fourth is indicative, because, manifestly, whatever happens on the fourth day will happen with exaggerated force on the seventh. The fifth day again is intercadent, and of no significance, nor is the sixth of any. The seventh is the first critical day, for then the moon is in quartile to the decumbiture, and is necessarily in a Sign of opposite nature in all respects to that in which she was at the decumbiture. If she was in Aries at the decumbiture, she will be on the seventh day in Cancer. Now, Aries is hot and dry, Cancer cold and moist; Aries is masculine, Cancer feminine; Aries diurnal, Cancer nocturnal. The quartile aspect is thus thoroughly hostile, and whatever process Luna favours at the decumbiture she will oppose when she reaches the quartile. At the decumbiture she favoured the disease, for otherwise the disease would not have occurred; at the quartile, therefore, she opposes the disease, and makes for a favourable crisis.

The eighth day is neutral, the ninth intercadent, the tenth neutral, and the eleventh indicative, for whatever happens on the eleventh will happen with exaggerated force on the fourteenth, which is the second and most critical day, for then the moon is in opposition to the decumbiture, and with all her might counteracts all that took place at the decumbiture. The next critical day is, of course, the twenty-first, when she is again in quartile, and finally, between the twenty-seventh and twenty-eighth she comes into conjunction. If the disease has not been ended by crisis on one of the three critical days, the reinforcement that it now receives from the conjunction of the moon converts the acute disease into a chronic, and henceforth it is governed no longer by the positions of the moon, but is regulated, according to the same laws, by the sun. The next crisis will not take place therefore for two months, when the sun will be in quartile to the decumbiture.

Of course, the favourable or unfavourable character of the crisis will depend largely upon whether, on the critical day, the moon is favourably aspected by good Planets, or unfavourably influenced by bad ones.

It will be seen that all of these influences and dates depend upon the moment of the decumbiture, which is described as the first punct of time of the invasion of the disease; and this, as Galen says, is very hard to find. It is easy, indeed, to find the decumbiture in the literal sense, that is to say, the time when the patient takes to his bed;

but when the beginning of the sickness is, that, says Culpeper, is the question ; 'for a lusty stout man bears the disease longer before he takes to his bed than a puny sickly man : a meer suspition of sicknesse will send a faint-hearted man to bed ; you may perswade him he is sick whether he is or no. Notwithstanding, in most acute diseases, as also in many others, as Falling Sickness, Palsies, Apoplexies, and Pleurisies, 'tis an easy thing to find the precise time of the invasion of a disease. The best opinion is that that moment of time is to be taken in which a man finds a manifest paine or hurt in his body ; for instance, when a man hath got a Fever, usually the head akes certain dayes before ; this is not the Fever, but a messenger or forerunner of the Fever ; the true beginning is when a horrour or trembling invades the Sick.'

Certain objections to these doctrines did not escape the notice of the astrologers who taught them. 'If,' says one, 'the crisis depends on the motion of the moon and her aspect to the other Planets, what is the reason, if two men be taken ill at one and the same time, that yet the crisis of one falls out well, and not so the other?' The reasons are manifold. The virtue working is changed according to the diversity of the virtue receiving; for you all know the sun makes the clay hard and the wax soft, it makes the cloth white and the face black; so then, if one be a child, whose nature is hot and moist, the other a man in the prime of life, whose nature is hot and dry, and the third an old man, whose nature is cold and dry, the crisis works diversely because their natures are different.

Secondly, in the Spring time, diseases are most obnoxious to a child, because his nature is hot and moist. A disease works most violently with a choleric man in Summer, with a melancholy man in Autumn, and with a phlegmatic man in Winter.

Thirdly, if at the decumbiture the moon was aspected by Mars, whose nature is hot and dry, if the disease be of heat and drought it is mightily aggravated: not so if it be cold.

Fourthly, the complexions of the patients may be different; the one hot and dry, the other cold and moist. If the disease be hot and dry, it will not be so violent upon a cold and moist body as on a hot and dry.

Fifthly, their nativities may not agree. If the moone be aspected by Saturne or Mars at the nativity, the disease is dangerous; not so if she be aspected by Jupiter or Venus; or Saturn may be Lord of one nativity and not of the other, and then he may hurt the one and not the other, for the Devil will not hurt his own. If you can possibly get the nativities, you shall not err. 'For example, I know,' says my authority, 'three children born at one and the same time. At five years of age they all three had convulsion, whereby they were all three lame of one leg, the boyes on the right, and the girl on the left. At 14 they dyed altogether on one and the same day of the small pox.'

To us, with our present knowledge, and requirements of evidence, and our ways of thought, all this appears such a farrago of tomfoolery that it is difficult to understand how it can have been seriously entertained by men of ordinary intelligence; and yet we know that it was in fact believed by the rarest intellects of their time, some of them, like Roger Bacon and Albertus Magnus, among the rarest intellects of all time; and it is an interesting exercise to try and carry our minds back and put ourselves as far as we can in the position of our forefathers. We shall then find it easy to understand why the system was maintained, and not difficult to discover how it originated. The first is explained by the overwhelming power of authority, the last by the belief that was overthrown by Copernicus.

In the first place, we must imagine ourselves living on an earth that is the centre of the universe, and that to the earth, and especially to its human inhabitants, the rest of the universe is subservient. The universe was created to serve a certain purpose, 'the diapason closing full in man.' That anything could exist for any other purpose than the service of mankind was not conceived, was probably not conceivable, by our forefathers. At a time almost within the memory of some now living, one of our leading philosophers declared that in the world there is nothing great but man. If he had expressed all that was in his mind, no doubt he would have said in the world there is nothing great but Scotchmen; but taking the declaration as he made it, it summarises effectively the attitude of our ancestors towards the cosmos. It was made for their benefit. To them there was no greater paradox than that

Full many a gem of purest ray serene
  The dark, unfathomed caves of ocean bear,
Full many a flower is born to blush unseen,
  And waste (mark the word) its sweetness on the desert air.

This being so, of what use are the heavenly bodies? The overpowering and incalculable value to man of the sun is evident enough. By its daily transit through the sky it makes the difference between the day, the time of man's activity, and night, the time of his repose. By its annual transit through the Signs of the Zodiac it makes the differences among the seasons, and so regulates his food supply, whether animal or vegetable, his comfort, and his welfare in a thousand particulars. Here we have the root of the whole matter; but to understand it fully we must remember that the sun was but one of seven Planets, all resembling him in so many important respects that it was impossible not to attribute to them powers corresponding with his, if different from his. So that, if the sun had power over the affairs of men, so had the other Planets; if his power varied according to the Sign he occupied, so did theirs; if his power altered with his height above the horizon, so did theirs. In a world in which natural law was unknown, and everything seemed to happen by chance, the mind clutched at anything that offered an explanation of the ways in which things happen. Here was an explanation ready to hand, and needing only study and interpretation.

The moon is evidently complementary to the sun. Her power is greatest when she is in opposition, and at this time she antagonises the sun by producing a colourable imitation of daylight at night, and thus interfering with his power of regulating light and darkness. This is naturally taken as an instance of a general law, that opposition means antagonism, a meaning that is now become fixed and general; and since opposition is but one of several differences of position, it follows that every such difference—trine, quartile and sextile—means some difference of influence. Again, the moon, as far as her power extends, antagonises the sun, and works against him. But the sun is manifestly and immensely beneficial to the human race, and is a benevolent power; consequently, the moon is malevolent and injurious. Both sun and moon are but samples and members of the family of Planets, and whatever characters they possess must be shared by the rest of the family. The other Planets, therefore, must be benevolent or malevolent in their degree, and must exercise their powers, as the sun and moon do, according to their position above the horizon, that is in the Houses of Heaven, or in the Signs of the Zodiac.

As the sun undoubtedly by its position and movements produces the seasons, and as the moon has faculties and qualities of like kind, though inferior in power, it follows that she too regulates some natural phenomena of minor importance to the seasons. Such minor natural phenomena are displayed by the weather; and the belief that the moon regulates the weather is the one astrological doctrine that still displays vitality. The other Planets are irregular in their movements, being now rapid, now slow, now direct, now retrograde; clearly, therefore, their influence will be exerted upon those great natural events that are irregular and occasional in their incidence; and thus it is that Saturn produces intense frost, inundations and tempests; that Mars regulates thunder and lightning and the invasion of pirates; that Venus brings beneficial floods, rains, and mists; that under Mercury occur droughts and squalls, and so forth.

All these catastrophes have their effects on the welfare and fortunes of men, and consonantly with the belief already stated, were conclusively presumed to take place for no other purpose than to affect, in one direction or other, the lives and fortunes of men. It would be strange if, after being credited with these powers for this purpose, the Planets were not further endowed with the power of causing those catastrophes, equally inexplicable otherwise, and still more affecting human welfare, plague, pestilence, and all other diseases.

In order to produce diseases, the Planets must influence the humours by whose defect or excess diseases were produced; and since *entia non sunt multiplicanda praeter necessitatem*, the Planets could not influence these humours except by themselves possessing and distributing the same elementary qualities, heat, cold, drought, and moisture, that characterise the humours. This doctrine was the easier to establish since it was already known that these four qualities pervade all things in nature. The very elements themselves, out of which all things are compounded, are but embodiments of the four elementary qualities in their four possible combinations. Fire is hot and dry, Air is hot and moist, Earth is cold and dry, Water is cold and moist. When it is remembered that the four humours are similarly compounded, yellow bile being hot and dry, blood hot and moist, black bile cold and dry, and phlegm cold and moist, it becomes evident, even if it were not already certain from the universal prevalence of these qualities, that corresponding pairs must be possessed by the several Planets to give them those powers over disease that they undoubtedly exercise. This useful method of the *circulus in probando* is not the only device that our forefathers have bequeathed to us, and that still serves our purposes with all its original efficacy.

When we have got thus far, the remaining doctrines of medical astrology follow naturally by the development and elaboration of those we already possess, aided by further analogies, more or less far-fetched, and by chance coincidences, such as that already mentioned which led Guy de Chauliac to attribute the great plague of 1345 to the conjunction of Saturn, Jupiter and Mars in Aquarius in March of that year.

We should take a very superficial view of Astrology, however, if we failed to recognise that beneath all its strange doctrines, and under all its monstrous assumptions, lies the insatiable craving of the human mind for explanation. Every event that happens before us throws down an irresistible challenge to us to explain it. We are so constituted that we cannot rest until it is explained; but we are also so constituted that we are apt to accept as sufficient anything that purports to be an explanation, even if it rests upon no reasonable ground, or even if it is a mere verbal explanation that explains nothing. We have discarded Astrology as a garment that we have outgrown, even as the snake wriggles itself out of its skin, and the crab withdraws itself from a rigid envelope that is too small for it; but can we assure ourselves that we have outgrown and discarded the mental carapace that renders such beliefs as Astrology possible? Do not logicians still teach doctrines every bit as absurd as the doctrines of Astrology? And even in Medicine itself, do we never take that for an explanation that is no explanation? Before we can cast stones at the Astrologers, have we no windows of our own to guard? Let those answer who explain aphasia by calling it a loss of memory for words; who explain ataxy by calling it loss of the power of coordinating movements; who explain a delusion by discovering a lesion in the brain; who explain feeble-mindedness by hereditary influence; who explain hysteria entertained in middle age by some sexual irregularity committed in youth; or who explain an hypothetical increase of appendicitis by an hypothetical increase in the consumption of meat. Surely we have every right to despise those who attributed all acute diseases to the influence of the moon, and all chronic diseases to the influence of the sun, for we know with assured knowledge that acute diseases are in fact produced by intestinal stasis, and that chronic diseases are due to that blessed combination of words—alimentary toxæmia.

ASTROLOGY IN MEDICINE.

To the Editor of THE LANCET.

SIR,—I trust that with your well-known love of fair play you will kindly permit me to make a few remarks on this subject and to ask Dr Mercier a few questions of public interest.

With all respect for the learned doctor, and with due acknowledgment of his candid admission that astrology was believed in and seriously studied 'by the rarest intellects of their time, some of them, like Roger Bacon and Albertus Magnus, the rarest intellects of all time,' I wish to ask: Does Dr Mercier think that such rarest intellects were incapable of distinguishing truth from error, and could have accepted the superstitions associated in their day with astrology? Surely not. They accepted *astrologia sana* as Bacon (Lord Verulam) accepted it, as a part of physics and discarded superstition. One might as reasonably proclaim medicine nowadays to be 'tomfoolery,' on the ground of the superstitions connected with it formerly, as Dr Mercier condemns astrology and pronounces it as 'dead'—officially. Dr Mercier's only argument against astrology on scientific grounds is the worn-out and utterly unfounded assertion that it was overthrown by Copernicus!

. . . .

Dr Mercier ridicules the belief of that eminent man Guy de Chauliac that the outbreak of the 'Black Death' in the middle of the fourteenth century was due to the great conjunction of Saturn, Jupiter, and Mars in *Aquarius* on March 24th, 1345. Neptune was also in the same sign at that time—a planet unknown then. Such a doryphory of great planets in *Aquarius*, a sign which is found to relate to epidemic diseases, certainly foreshadowed the outbreak of a pandemic; and if Dr Mercier will compare the periods of great conjunctions in Aquarius he will find that great epidemics always coincided therewith. If Dr Mercier had directed attention to the immense difference made by the discovery of Uranus and Neptune, he would have recognised that many mistakes of ancient and mediæval astrologers were due to their being unaware of the existence and relative positions of these distant planets.

I hope Dr Mercier will forgive me for directing attention to the above points. I am sure that he meant to be as fair as possible in his delineation of mediæval astrology; in fact, he proved this intention by the last paragraph but one of his second lecture. I should be happy to meet Dr Mercier in friendly debate on this important subject before any learned society or private assembly.

I am, Sir, yours faithfully,
ALFRED J. PEARCE.

Dec. 3rd, 1913.

*** Mr Pearce makes an appeal for publication which we have not been able to resist, but the view that the operations of nature are mysterious until they are understood cannot be advanced as a complete defence of mysticism.—ED. L.

To the Editor of THE LANCET.

SIR,—Like yourself, I am unable to withstand the appeal that Mr Pearce makes to me. He asks me whether I think that Roger Bacon and Albertus Magnus were incapable of distinguishing truth from error. I hasten to assure him that in my opinion these eminent men were as incapable of making a mistake as I am myself. The experience of mankind throughout the ages shows that clever men never make mistakes. No clever general has ever been defeated in battle; no clever judge was ever upset on appeal; no clever counsel ever lost a cause; no clever theologian ever held an erroneous opinion, or at any rate an opinion that was held to be erroneous by other clever theologians; no clever doctor ever made a wrong diagnosis; no clever schoolboy ever needs to have his exercises corrected; in fact ability and infallibility mean the same thing.

Mr Pearce is certainly right in pouring contempt upon my argument that Copernicus overthrew astrology; at least, he would have been right if I had made the statement, or if I had called it an argument.

I should be most happy to accept Mr Pearce's challenge to debate this important subject before a learned society were it not that I am at present immersed in a much more important investigation, which absorbs my whole time and attention. That Saturn, Jupiter, and Mars, in conjunction in Aquarius, must have produced the Black Death in the following year is patent to everyone and needs no demonstration, but it required the insight of genius to discover that the burning of York Minster was due to the superabundance of snails in a certain back garden early in the same year. It is the peculiar merit of the adept, be he an astrologer or merely an haruspex, to recognise the significance of such coincidences. It seems to have escaped altogether the observation of the vulgar that this year of grace 1913 has been characterised no less by the superabundance of snails in back gardens than by the number of conflagrations initiated by suffragettes. The causal nexus needs no proof; but if it did, proof would be found in the fact that in Ireland, from which snails were banished by the beneficent action of St Patrick, and where there are no back gardens, the backs of the houses being in front, there has been no suffragette incendiarism. I will not pursue the subject further in this place, but if Mr Pearce wants any further information he will find it in my forthcoming book, 'Dė Conflagrationibus et de Multitudinibus Helicidarum in Hortulis Posticis.'

I am, Sir, yours faithfully,

CHAS. MERCIER.

Dec. 13*th*, 1913.

SAINTS AND SIGNS

(Part of a third Lecture, which was not delivered, but was read to the Casual Club, *Nov.* 1912)

It used to be a point of honour with me, and I believe with other members of this Club, never to read up the subject of the evening's discussion. So to do would be to deprive the discussions of that casual character which is their distinctive charm, and which gives its name to the Club. It is with regret that I have noticed of late years signs that this honourable understanding is not maintained, and therefore I have chosen for this paper a title which will have rendered impracticable any attempt to acquire information of its subject from outside sources. If any member present has been trying to steal a march upon the rest by looking up the literature of miraculous signs, adduced in evidence of the truths of Christianity by the heroes or the victims of canonisation, I have the pleasure of informing him that he has been wasting his time; and I may further inform those members who have made direct inquiries of me as to the scope of the subject indicated by my title, that my answers, while of course strictly truthful, were intended to mislead, and have, I trust, served their purpose.

I have here a specimen of a metallic token, which, if any of you have never seen one, I shall be glad to hand round—I wish I had more, so that I might present one to each of you as a memento of this joyful occasion, but the Chancellor of the Exchequer seizes upon every specimen with such avidity that they are becoming more and more scarce and difficult to obtain—a metallic token which serves in this country as the standard of value, and is known as the sovereign or pound sterling. If you will let observation with extensive view survey it on both aspects, you will find that on the obverse or the reverse—I never know which is which—it bears the image, though not the superscription, of St George of Cappadocia, who has abandoned the more lucrative occupation of army contractor in order to follow the more honourable calling of patron saint.

He is engaged, you will observe, in his customary avocation of slaying the dragon, an operation which he performs in a rather surprising manner. Chastely attired in a helmet much too large for him, the weight of which has dislocated his neck, and mounted on a pony many sizes too small for him, the saint is in the act of kicking the dragon in the neck with his bare foot, while the pony simultaneously kicks the animal on the head with his off fore, and treads on its abdomen with his near hind. The triple assault so confounds the dragon that instead of biting the leg of the saint or of the pony, both of which are within easy reach, he retaliates by swearing, which any intelligent dragon must know would avail little against a Welsh pony (unless indeed the dragon should swear in Welsh, of which there is no evidence) and would be quite ineffectual against a saint, especially a saint who had had as long an experience in the army as St George of Cappadocia.

George of Cappadocia was a commercial man, and a very successful commercial man, and no doubt it is meet and right and our bounden duty to place upon the standard of value in this commercial country the effigy of a successful commercial man. But it is not on account of his success in commerce that the effigy of George appears on the fronts—or backs—of our coins. If we wanted to typify upon our coins the highest development of the commercial spirit, I suppose we should stamp them with the image of Lord Rothschild, or of Mr Rockefeller; but we do not. We stamp them with the image of St George of Cappadocia, not because he was a prosperous and successful commissary, but because, for some unknown reason, he subsequently became a saint. At some remote time, I do not know when or why, George was chosen as the patron saint of this country, and it is because he is the patron saint of England that his image appears on those useful tokens that are collected with such avidity by the Chancellor of the Exchequer. Mr Rockefeller would not be eligible, because he is not a saint.

Patron saints were in past times much more highly valued and much more frequently employed than they are now. France has, or had, a patron in St Louis. I speak without accurate knowledge, but I believe I am correct in saying that, in the common phrase, he has joined the ranks of the unemployed. Scotland placed itself under the patronage of St Andrew, Ireland of St Patrick, Wales of St David, Spain of St James; and if I cannot adduce any other examples, it is because these are the only nations—if we can allow that Scotland is a nation—that remain as they were before the modern redistribution of the map of Europe.

But nations were not the only things that had patron saints. Every family that aspired to county rank, and indeed, every person who aspired to be of consequence, had his or her patron saint. Nor was this all, as they say in Oxford. Every profession and calling had its patron saint. The patron saint of medicine was St Luke. Who was the patron saint of lawyers I do not know, but no doubt they chose a very powerful one, for their need was great; or perhaps no saint would consent to act for them, for of all the Inns of Court it is curious that not one is named after a saint. As to other callings, the sailor-men had a patron saint in St Botolph, ferrymen in St Christopher, fishermen in St Peter, shoemakers in St Crispin, butchers in St Bartholomew, huntsmen in St Hubert and so on. I need not remind you that to this day every church has its patron saint, but you may not know that every part of the human body, and every ailment of the human body had its patron saint.

The head was under the patronage of St Ottila; the neck acknowledged St Blasius; the body, St Lawrence; the legs and feet, St Rochus and St John; and thereby hangs a curious tale, as we shall see presently.

Except for countries and churches, patron saints are not now much utilised; but it is evident, from their universal employment in former times, that they were once of great importance. At the present day, a patron is a merely ornamental personage. He gives his name, and he is usually expected to give a subscription, but beyond this, his only function is to confer respectability. In former times, however, his functions were much more active. Patron, I may remind you, is correlative with client, as father with child, or master with servant. A child necessarily implies a father, and without a father can no child be. A master implies a servant, and where there is a servant, there there must be a master. And similarly, patron and client are correlative. There can be no patron without a client, and no client without a patron. For this reason, I object to and resent the custom that has recently arisen, of tradesmen calling their customers clients, especially as in the same breath they ask their customers for patronage. A master might as well ask his servant for orders, or a father expect a tip from his child, as a patron ask his client for patronage.

The relation of patron and client was the relation of protector and protected. I don't know whether those who placed themselves under the patronage of a saint called themselves his clients, but undoubtedly they invoked and expected his protection; and it was for the sake of protection that they provided themselves with patron saints. We must remember that in the days when men provided themselves with patron saints, no one could afford to be without protection. We have only to pay attention to the litany to realise how urgent was the need. The litany is one long prayer for protection. We pray to be protected from evil and mischief, from the crafts and assaults of the devil, from the wrath of God, from lightning and tempest, from plague, pestilence and famine, from battle and murder, and from sudden death. We pray for protection for all that travel by land or by water, for all prisoners and captives, for all sick persons (against their doctors I suppose), and for all sorts and conditions of men.

In those days, the modern conception of the reign of law, in the sense of the inexorableness of natural causation, had not yet been attained. Things happened in those days, not in obedience to natural laws, but according to caprice, and to whether the devil got a chance when God was not attending, or when the saints, his ministers, were pre-occupied with other affairs. The Almighty was too august to be approached directly. Indeed, it seems to have been assumed that he occupied the position of a constitutional sovereign, and acted only on the advice or the intercession of his ministers, the saints, so that it was of the first importance to have the protection and favour of a powerful and influential saint.

When clans or nations joined battle, their war-cry was the name of their patron saint, who was expected to fight on the side of his votaries or clients, to see that they had all the luck and came out top dog. Not infrequently, the saint came down on purpose, and in bodily presence led them to the attack. Many such instances are on record, and it is worth notice that, whoever the saint that thus interpreted his obligations, he was always mounted on a white horse.

Although wars were very frequent in mediæval times, it would be a mistake to suppose, as historians before the present generation seemed to suppose, that the whole time of the whole male population of the world was occupied in fighting, and in nothing else. No doubt, in times when there were no newspapers, no novels, no theatres, no cricket, no football, no suffragists, no divorce court, no kinematographs and no parliamentary debates, people must have suffered terrible boredom, and would have been driven now and then to do a little wholesome fighting from sheer vacancy of mind; and no doubt, when there were no motor buses, no taxi-cabs and no municipal tram-cars, the normal increase of population must have required some other check to keep it within the bounds of the means of subsistence; and so people plunged into war to save themselves from famine; but still, the laity did not live wholly on acorns and beech-mast, nor the clergy on Greek roots, and therefore some industrial occupations must have been followed; and we know as a matter of fact that some were followed; and whatever a man's occupation might be, whether of war or peace, it was necessary, if he was to have any luck, that he should have a patron saint; and hence it was that a patron saint presided over every trade and calling. Not even thieving could prosper except under the patronage of St Nicholas.

My own occupation had not then reached the perfection that it has now attained, and in those days there were maladies that baffled the resources of medical art as it then was, and defied all the drugs in the pharmacopœia, reinforced as that then was by many potent and valuable remedies that the ignorance and indifference of a later age has suffered to fall into disuse. Pounded earthworms, ants' eggs, asses' dung, the urine of a bull or—strange alternative—of a virgin, vipers' fat, the water that had been used for washing a corpse—all these, incredible as it appears, sometimes failed to cure; and then there was no resource left but to go to the celestial Harley Street, and consult a specialist saint. For the celestial Harley Street had as many saintly specialists as its mundane successor has now of specialists who are, perhaps, not altogether saintly. St Apollonius was the leading authority on toothache; St Avertin appropriated my own specialty of lunacy; St Benedict practised in stone and other diseases of the bladder; St Hubert specialised in hydrophobia; St John in epilepsy; St Vitus in chorea; St Maur in gout; and St Anthony in erysipelas. Of course, it was not to be expected that everyone should know the right saint to go to in any particular malady, any more than the man in the street knows at the present time precisely the best specialist, who is not a saint, to consult for the malady with which he may happen to be afflicted. It would have been as absurd to go for one's gout to St Apollonius, the President, if one may so put it, of the celestial College of Dentists, as for the toothache to St Maur, whose specialty was gout. In cases of difficulty, it was necessary to consult a priest, as one now consults a general practitioner.

Of course, in those days as in these, the fee had to be considered. Guineas had not then been coined, and payment was usually made in candles, burnt at the shrine of the saint, a mode of remuneration that, for my own part, I am glad to say has been abandoned. This method of payment was rather after that of the sister profession than of modern medicine. The saint had a number of candles marked on his brief, as it were, and unless the retainer was satisfactory, he refused to look at the papers. No doubt there were needy saints, not too scrupulous, who would undertake any case for a candle or two, whether they were qualified to treat it or not; just as now there are sixpenny doctors, and surgeons who will undertake a case of mental disease; but it is to be hoped that the leaders of the profession had more conscience, and that a saint who specialised on blindness, for instance, would no more undertake a dislocation or a fracture than a Chancery leader would undertake the defence of a prisoner at the Old Bailey, or a reputable surgeon would treat a patient suffering from mental disorder.

So far, then, our mediaeval ancestors were thoroughly well provided with patrons. There was scarcely any occasion in life that had not a saint who had specialised in its requirements and was ready to supply them for a consideration —for a sufficient number of candles. But it is evident that such a complete equipment of saints could not have been suddenly, nor even rapidly constituted. It must have been the growth of years and of generations; and moreover, we must remember that there was a time, at the beginning of the Christian era, when, though sins were very many, saints were very few, and until the large additions made to the noble army of martyrs in the reign of Diocletian, there could not possibly have been saints enough to go round; and if we go further back, and recede from the penumbra of early A.D. to the outer darkness of B.C., we enter a benighted world in which there were no saints at all. The prospect appals! We might almost as well contemplate a world in which there were no barristers. The question presents itself, and presses upon us with irresistible force—What did our unhappy ancestors do in a world in which there were no saints? It is clear that patrons or protectors of some kind they must have had, for in pre-Christian, no more than in mediaeval times, was there any conviction or knowledge of the operation of natural laws. How do we know this? We have it on unexceptionable authority. A contemporary writer, who is generally believed to have been inspired, asserts 'He hath not dealt so with any nation, neither have the heathen any knowledge of his laws.' Consequently, there was the same lack of any rule or governance in the happening of events. Everything went by chance, according as the devil or the saints were paying attention, or got the upper hand at the moment. But there were no saints. Hence it would appear that the devil must have had it all his own way, and that the affairs of men must have been uniformly and invariably unfortunate. But they were not, for man survived. He not only survived, but he prospered and flourished. He increased and multiplied exceedingly. Men organised themselves into great nations, built great cities, and were subject to mighty kings. Egypt, Nineveh, Babylon, Assyria, Persia, the Empire of India and the greater Empire of China, all attest that, long before there were saints to interest themselves in him, man succeeded, somehow or other, in antagonising the devil and getting the better of him. It is of the utmost interest and importance to discover how he did this, and what were the means that he employed; and this brings me to the middle of my song, and the second part of my paper. I am now done with Saints. It is clear that they were not as indispensable as they made themselves out; and—I say it with reluctance, but—I have grave doubts whether they did not lay claim, if not to powers they did not possess, at any rate to the exclusive possession of powers by no means peculiar to them. We know, indeed, that on one historical occasion, St Dunstan did seize the devil by the nose with a pair of tongs; and we are told, on less unimpeachable authority, but we are told, that St Nicholas kicked him on a place which is described as being near the spot where the tail joins on to the small of the back; but with these exceptions, though he was constantly outwitted, and indeed he appears to be a kind of Simple Simon, easily gulled by the most transparent device, and no more astute than the victims of the confidence trick—with these exceptions, I say, there are few, if any, records of personal encounters with the devil till we come down to Martin Luther; and Martin Luther was not a saint. He was never, I understand, canonised, and I am informed on good authority, in reply to inquiry made in the highest quarters, that any application to Rome for his canonisation would have little or no chance of success.

Still, whatever unaccountable prejudices may exist at Rome against the canonisation of this great and good man, I cannot see that we are any nearer a solution of the most important, and indeed vital question, What did men do for patrons before they had saints to fly to? This, gentlemen, is the great and epoch-making discovery that I have to announce to you on this memorable evening. This is the brilliant result of years of laborious research. This is the golden fruit of a lifetime of very insufficiently rewarded toil. Why should I repine that the paltry metal counters that I exhibited at the beginning of this address are so scarce and rare, when I have garnered so abundantly rewards so much more precious? What did men do for patronage and protection before they had saints to place themselves under? Why, this was what they did. Not to keep you in suspense any longer, I will at once reveal that they sought the protection of the Signs of the Zodiac and of the Planets; and as far as it is possible to judge, the protection they obtained therefrom was as ample, as efficient, and as abundant, as that of all the saints in the calendar.

Many centuries before a single saint had been canonised, the system of patronage by the heavenly bodies was completely organised—was, if I may so put it, in full swing; and all the Christian hagiology did was to adopt this system, ousting the heavenly bodies, and filling their places with saints. Long before St Louis, or St Andrew, or that successful commissary St George, was born or thought of, every nation and city of antiquity had its patron Sign. Every calling had its own patron Sign or Planet; every part of the body its patron Sign or Planet: and every illness had a double process of cure, being remediable not only by certain drugs, but according to the position and movement of the Planets among the Signs when the drugs were collected and when they were administered. The series of saints and the series of Signs present a complete parallel, and it is evident that in this as in other things Christianity took advantage of a pre-existing organisation and adapted it to its own uses. It took the institution of patronage by celestial personages, as it took the institution of periodical festivals; emptied them of their previous contents, and filled them with Christian matter, leaving the pagan form unaltered. Thus it took the great annual winter festival, and altered it arbitrarily to Christmas day, pretending that it is the anniversary of the birth of Christ, for which there is not one tittle of evidence; but it could not, or did not, alter the minor weekly festival which still has its name from the greatest of the Planets. In these cases the supersession was either complete or none at all, but in other matters, and especially in the matter of patronage and protection, the struggle was very prolonged, and for ages the two systems of patronage existed side by side; and alongside the priests, who were experts in advising as to the appropriate saint to invoke, were the astrologers, experts in advising the proper conjunction or disposition of the heavenly bodies to wait for before beginning any undertaking or altering any course of action, and also for the purpose of determining whether a course of action was or was not judicious, and calculated to be successful. Between the two sets of practitioners there was a natural jealousy. The Church forbad recourse being had to the aid of Astrology, and threatened excommunication to anyone who consulted the rival expert, just as at present the orthodox physician boycotts the homœopath. On the other hand the astrologer, who was often an infidel, often a Jew or an Arab, despised and ridiculed the pretensions of the saints. Whatever faith, or want of faith, either sect had in its own ministrations, neither was without an uneasy feeling that the other might, after all, have something in it. The astrologers were not above invoking the aid of the saints in their own personal difficulties, and the very Popes who issued bulls fulminating against Astrology and its practitioners, yet kept their own private astrologers, whom they consulted on the sly. In spite of their mutual antagonism, however, the two systems existed side by side for many centuries, and neither can boast of a complete triumph over the other. Astrology is dead, it is true, but in Protestant countries the invocation of saints perished long before its rival, and the influence of the heavenly bodies was consulted by very many who would have scorned to invoke a saint.

Very many days in the year had their patron saints, and those who are familiar with old chronicles know that the date of an event was never signalised by the day of the month, but always by the saint's day that it fell upon, or, in the few cases in which the day had not been appropriated by some saint or other, the date was signalised as being on the eve of the day following, which was sure to have its patron saint, or the morrow of the previous day. Correspondingly, every day of the week had its patron Planet. The number seven was chosen for the days of the week, no doubt because in seven days the moon completes a quarter, and in 28 days completes its revolution. By a curious coincidence, the number of Planets known to the ancient world was also seven, and hence it was natural that to every Planet should be assigned one day in the week. By an easy transition, made at a time that I have not been able to identify, but that was certainly very early, the powers of the Planets and those of the gods became transferable, and with the powers the names, so that only three of the seven days of the week, Saturday, Sunday, and Monday, are known by the names of Planets, the remaining four being called after the corresponding gods.

As with days, so with other things. We have seen that to some saint or other every part of the body was apportioned; and similarly the body was carved up and portioned out among the Signs of the Zodiac, as we find in the chapter of Arnaldus de Villanova, *De quolibet signo quod membrum in corpore respicit,* and as is set forth in the first lecture in this book, so that it is clear that the heathen had as good a choice of celestial specialists as ever the Christians had.

Time fails me to carry out the parallel in further detail, but just as the patron Sign of England is St George, and the effigy of St George appears upon our coins, so the patron Sign of Syria was Aries, and the effigy of the Ram appears on Syrian coins. Similarly, Palmyra was under the patronage of Libra, and on the coins of Palmyra appears the Balance. Similarly, individuals had their patron Signs before ever they had their patron saints. The patron Sign of Augustus was Capricorn, of Pythodeia Queen of Pontus, the Balance. The custom continued well into mediæval times and into Christian countries, and King Stephen of England adopted and placed on his coins the patron Sign of Sagittarius.

CAMBRIDGE: PRINTED BY JOHN CLAY, M.A. AT THE UNIVERSITY PRESS